BRADY

BRADY

LIFE LESSONS
FROM A LEGEND

BRIAN BOONE

CASTLE POINT BOOKS
NEW YORK

To Danny, who fulfilled his brotherly duties in teaching me the rules of football and always letting me play with his collection of little plastic NFL helmets.

—B.B.

ISBN 978-1-250-28533-1 (paper over board)
ISBN 978-1-250-28534-8 (ebook)

Design by Katie Jennings Campbell
Composition by Noora Cox
Illustrations by Gilang Bogy

Our books may be purchased in bulk for promotional, educational, or business use.
Please contact your local bookseller or the Macmillan Corporate and Premium
Sales Department at 1-800-221-7945, extension 5442,
or by email at MacmillanSpecialMarkets@macmillan.com.

First Edition: 2023

10 9 8 7 6 5 4 3 2 1

"IF YOU WANT TO PERFORM AT THE HIGHEST LEVEL, THEN YOU HAVE TO PREPARE AT THE HIGHEST LEVEL."

CONTENTS

INTRODUCTION

Tom Brady is pro football's "G.O.A.T."—the greatest of all time—not just for offensive players or quarterbacks, but of anyone who has ever suited up and played in an NFL game. Nobody has ever played in more Super Bowls, won more Super Bowls, started more games at the quarterback position, or so consistently delivered in the clutch as Brady. His achievements on the field in the regular season and postseason are staggering, eclipsing past and contemporary quarterbacks alike.

In his first 22 seasons (a record for longevity for a starting QB), Brady has led his teams to 18 division titles, 17 with the New England Patriots and one with the Tampa Bay Buccaneers. In that period, Brady never had a losing season. He's the NFL's all-time leader in wins, touchdown passes, passing yards, and completed passes. He's also the NFL's all-time leader in postseason wins, passing yards, and touchdown passes. Brady has been named the NFL's most valuable player three times and won the Super Bowl seven times. That's more than any other pro football player ever, and more than any other NFL *franchise*.

Brady was the MVP of football's title game five times, another unmatched accomplishment. Brady is also the only quarterback to ever throw more than 5,200 yards in a season more than once, and one of those times he was 44 years old, well past the usual football player retirement age.

He's the kind of player who gets the job done—not just in clutch moments—but all game long, all season long, and for his whole two-plus decades career.

This level of success and achievement may seem like it was in the cards all along, thanks to Brady's natural gifts. But a Hall of Fame-level career full of memorable moments and astounding feats of athleticism didn't just fall into Brady's lap. It happened through a lot of work, unfailing dedication, and a steadfast willingness to learn, adapt, evolve, try, and push himself. Football glory was never predestined or even predicted for a young Brady; he was a high school benchwarmer who wasn't highly recruited, who had to fight for his spot on a college squad, and who was drafted in a very low round by a team that planned to employ him as a seldom-used backup to a star quarterback. But Tom

"IF YOU DON'T PLAY TO WIN, DON'T PLAY AT ALL."

Brady was ready to go whenever the opportunity arose, and he routinely rose to the occasion and showed the world—and himself—what he was capable of accomplishing.

Tom Brady's guiding principles are universal.

Through careful planning, fortitude, and discipline, he's achieved his initial dreams and then some. How he's lived his life, and carried himself, on the field and off, is a worthy example for anyone trying to meet their own goals and aspirations. The rules Brady lives by and plays by are yours for the taking. They lay out a solid road map for success in any pursuit.

SUCCESS WAS ALWAYS THE PLAN

In an English essay Tom Brady wrote in high school (and recently posted online), he shared a surprisingly accurate vision of his future. He wrote, "I will continue to flourish in life as well as in athletics because of my strong will to succeed and desire to always be on top."

PINPOINT YOUR PASSION

CHAPTER 1

Sometimes it takes people years or even decades before they realize what they want to pursue. Others recognize their strengths and talents early, and they set out on their journeys at a relatively young age. Tom Brady, for example, knew he wanted to be a football player from the time he was a teenager. That's because he *loved* football. It ignited a passion for a life in sports; a passion so strong that it propelled him forward to become the greatest quarterback to ever throw a pass.

What also sets Brady apart from other football players, and other people who achieved all they set out to do, was that he didn't stop. Once he got to the NFL and won a Super Bowl, he didn't rest on his laurels. He never stopped winning, and always challenged himself to go farther than others thought possible. Brady's long-range perspective

"THE ONLY THING I EVER WANTED TO BE WAS A PROFESSIONAL FOOTBALL PLAYER."

made him the longest-playing quarterback and most-awarded champion in NFL history.

NURTURE YOUR INNER COMPETITOR

Born in 1977, Thomas Edward Patrick Brady Jr. was raised in the wealthy San Francisco Bay Area town of San Mateo. His father, Thomas Brady Sr., worked in insurance and eventually started his own firm, Thomas Brady and Associates. It still exists, with many branch offices around the US, and it allowed Tom Sr. and his wife, Galynn, economic comfort for their family. Galynn quit her job working for the airline industry in order to raise her four children: daughters Maureen, Nancy, and Julie; and son Tom Jr.

Tom Brady's household was as tight-knit as it was competitive and sports-centric. Tom Sr. was an avid golfer and skier who engaged in one of those two activities almost every weekend, depending on the season. Meanwhile, all of the young Brady women were elite team sport athletes. Maureen was so good at softball that she attended Fresno State University and pitched on the USA Softball Junior Olympics team. Nancy Brady earned a softball scholarship to UC Berkeley, and Julie went to college on a scholarship for her soccer skills. Tom Brady Sr. later recalled that, according to the family calendar, the Bradys once had 315 games in total in one year. And the siblings attended every one of each other's games, if they didn't get in the way of their own.

Tom Brady's sisters were so famous and renowned in and around San Mateo for their athletic accomplishments that their brother sometimes felt overlooked. Known as "the little Brady" by his extended family and friends, he didn't find the sport that would define him and hold his interest until he was a teenager. But he actively sought out some kind of passion and his purpose years earlier. In the ninth grade, he wrote "The Way My Sisters Influenced Me," an essay for his English composition class at Junipero Sierra High School, an upper-class, private, parochial school. In the essay, he made a prediction that it would be him who would one day be a household name. Brady used the good-natured rivalry and competitive spirit that fueled his family to motivate himself to accomplish big things, bigger things than anyone else in his family:

"Everything we did, and I mean everything, running home from church, everything was a competition. I guess it made things really fun, at least for the winner."

While he was proud of his sisters, he didn't want to live in their shadows forever.

FIND YOUR NICHE, OR LET IT FIND YOU

At first, Tom Brady thought he'd found his sport. Similar to how two of his sisters excelled in softball, in high school, Brady was a terrific baseball player. He played catcher, but was also a power hitter who could hit thundering home runs out of the stadium. However, Brady hadn't pinpointed his life's passion; he'd only found something at which he was naturally gifted. While he worked hard at the sport, he didn't feel the deep-down drive to make

"ONE DAY I'M GOING TO BE A HOUSEHOLD NAME."

WITNESSING HISTORY

Three-year-old Tom Brady was present at the 1981 NFC Championship game in San Francisco where Montana threw "the Catch" to Dwight Clark to defeat the Dallas Cowboys.

baseball his focus, a crucial element of future success in any discipline or activity. But baseball did demonstrate his incredible throwing accuracy, as well as tremendous arm strength, not to mention the ability to endure a collision—skills that would be just as valuable, if not more, in a quarterback.

Unlike many other professional athletes who plug into organized programs early on so they can enter the pros in their late teens or early twenties, Brady didn't play organized football until age fourteen. His parents wouldn't let him join any earlier. They thought football, with its tackling and hits, was too rough of a sport for a pre-adolescent child, particularly a child like Brady, who was thin and wiry, not big, tall, and muscular like the other youth football players he'd be facing.

Regardless, Brady developed not only a love for football, but an appreciation and ever-increasing

"I WAS ALWAYS FAIRLY SELF-MOTIVATED, AND MY PARENTS JUST OPENED THE DOOR FOR ME."

"WHEN I WAS A KID,
I'D BE IN THE PARKING LOT
AT CANDLESTICK [PARK],
THROWING THE FOOTBALL
WITH MY FRIENDS.
NOW I'M THROWING
TO THE BEST ATHLETES
IN THE WORLD, AND THEN
GETTING PAID FOR IT."

working knowledge of it. His family happened to be season ticket holders for the local NFL team, the San Francisco 49ers. In the 1980s, when Brady was growing up in Northern California, the 49ers went to multiple Super Bowls led by quarterback Joe Montana, who Brady would later say was his football idol.

LEARN THE VALUE OF HARD WORK

And so, Brady waited as long as he had to play football. While organized youth sports can teach many skills and impart qualities— including personal responsibility, how to be accountable to a team, and physical fitness—Brady learned to value those things before he

"YOUR LIFE WILL BE WHAT YOU MAKE OF IT."

"THIS ISN'T A JOB. IT'S REALLY A TRUE LOVE AND I FELL IN LOVE WITH WHAT I'M DOING A LONG TIME AGO."

ever joined a football team. His family regularly attended services at a Roman Catholic church, and Brady helped out during those masses as an altar boy. He also worked. At age twelve, Brady secured a job delivering newspapers around San Mateo. His mother would drive the family van slowly down the streets while "the little Brady" would lean out the back and throw rolled-up papers to their intended destination, honing his pinpoint passing abilities that would serve him well in football.

Each summer growing up in the 1980s, Tom Brady spent several weeks at the Minnesota dairy farm run by the Johnsons, his maternal grandparents. His chief duty: to milk cows under his grandfather's watchful eye. If Brady's milking missed the bucket and a few drops landed on the ground, Grandpa Johnson would remind his grandson that lost milk meant lost money and wasted effort. It's a lesson that clearly resonated with Brady, who grew up to be the kind of person who valued hard work and didn't waste any chances afforded him.

PATIENCE IS KEY

Perhaps Tom Brady's most signature and enduring quality is his competitive edge. He is relentlessly driven to win, and that desire inspires everything he does. Even before he played football, he was intensely devoted to winning, sometimes overly so. He frequently played golf with his father on Sunday mornings in the spring and summer. They'd bet on games with each other—Tom Sr. putting up money and Tom Jr. offering a certain number of car washes. Young Brady got so frustrated when he'd hit a bad shot that he was known to throw his clubs, and on one occasion, even broke one over his knee. When his sports-related temper flared up, Tom Sr. ended the game and made Tom Jr. cool down and be alone with his thoughts.

Finally, in 1991, in his freshman year, Tom Brady's parents allowed him to play football. He successfully tried out for Junipero Serra's football program, and landed a spot on the freshman team. He wasn't fast enough to be a wide receiver,

tough enough to be a running back, or physically large enough to play on the defensive line, so Brady and his keen throwing arm landed the prime spot of quarterback. More specifically, he landed the spot of *backup* quarterback. He spent the entire season on the bench without so much as a snap in a single game. Not only did Brady suffer from frustration and disappointment that season, but so did his team. They finished with a record of 0-8 with a single tie. Not one touchdown all season. It bothered him enough to write about it in his school essay:

> *"We've got to keep working out. I never want to have another losing season like that."*

PICK A PATH AND DON'T LOOK BACK

Brady's path as an athlete could have gone in a very different direction. His high school, Junipero Sierra, has one of the most respected and storied baseball programs in the United States. All-time Major League Baseball home run king Barry Bonds was a star there, as were future big-league standouts like Jim Fregosi and Gregg Jefferies. Also on that list: Tom Brady.

As a catcher for the varsity team, Brady helped his team clinch a California state baseball title, was invited to work out with the Seattle Mariners (whom he impressed by hitting a home run with a wood bat), and was drafted by the Montreal Expos. Brady feasibly could've entered professional baseball immediately after high school—but he didn't want to. He didn't love baseball as much as he loved football, a sport he wasn't naturally good at.

Despite his lack of opportunity and success in his first year of football, something had been unlocked in Brady. His deep and abiding love for football, and his willingness to do

anything to make a team and be a vital part of it, would grow and never falter.

Brady impressed his coaches so much with his work ethic and tenacity that in tenth grade, he won a spot on Junipero Sierra's junior varsity football team as the second-ranked quarterback on the depth chart behind the similarly promoted QB from the previous year. Through a twist of good fortune, Brady got the job of starting quarterback when his teammate decided he no longer wanted to play football. Finally, Brady was on a team where he was guaranteed significant playing time.

He was an explosive presence from that day onward, having trained and practiced for months awaiting his shot. He kicked off his first scrimmage by launching a 60-yard touchdown pass. In his first game,

Brady led the team to a game-winning drive in its final moments. Later that year, they went to the state championship game and lost only in the last few minutes on a drive by their opponents. It was never going to be an easy road if he continued on in the high-pressure role of quarterback with its ups and downs. He would later describe how exhausting it could be:

> *"It's a frustrating game because the situations so drastically change at different times over the course of the week, the game, the season. It feels like brain surgery at times."*

Despite the challenges innate in the game and the disappointments he knew he'd face as a quarterback, Brady knew it was his destiny.

THERE'S ALWAYS SOMETHING TO WORK ON

Proving his talents, leadership, clutch play, and strong arm on the junior varsity squad, Tom Brady was being eyed for the starting quarterback of the Junipero Sierra varsity team, the top team at the school. But he wasn't guaranteed the spot. His coach, Tom MacKenzie, had concerns about weak spots in Brady's skill set, specifically speed and agility, qualities that a

"THE ONLY THING I CARE ABOUT IS, 'AM I THE BEST I CAN BE?'"

successful quarterback needs to have in spades. So, in the summer after his sophomore year, Brady worked on developing faster footwork, becoming more agile, and getting stronger and more athletic overall. To improve his fitness and strength, he started lifting weights and developed a rigorous jump-rope regimen that the entire football team eventually adopted.

MacKenzie used the Five-Dot Drill to improve the fitness of the entire team. Five round marks are drawn or placed on the ground, and the player steps on the dots in different variations as quickly as possible, which builds agility and speed. Brady would do the Five-Dot Drill at practice, and then he'd repeat it at home. He was so devoted to getting his spot on the team and keeping it and so dedicated to

improvement that he spray-painted the five dots on his family's garage floor and ran the drill by himself, for hours, all summer long, and after football practices in the fall. To develop his throwing arm (which was already getting a lot of attention at this point), Brady stayed late at practices for one-on-one training. After that, he'd come home for dinner, go to the gym, and then head back home for more Five-Dot Drills.

Preparation and practice helped build Brady into a champion. All of his self-directed improvement plans worked. In both his junior and senior years of high school, he held the job of starting varsity quarterback for the Junipero Serra Padres. In those two years, he compiled 3,500 passing yards, 32 touchdowns, and an 11-9 record.

"I DIDN'T COME IN WITH THE OPPORTUNITY TO PLAY RIGHT AWAY. I HAD TO EARN IT."

In a senior year game against Sacred Heart Cathedral, he threw for 331 yards. Unfortunately, on the opposing seven-yard line with seconds left, he threw an interception that was returned for a touchdown. It was quite possibly the biggest loss of his career. Still, he was the team's MVP in his senior season despite a 5-5 record. Brady was named to the All-League Team and several other regional best-of squads, including All-State and All-Far West.

BE PERSISTENT

By the time he wrapped up high school, the formerly scrawny and underdeveloped Tom Brady stood at 6 feet 4 inches, weighed 212 pounds of mostly muscle, and had earned a reputation in California for his winning record, impressive stats, and the praise he drew from sportswriters and college scouts for his strength, accuracy, and quick release. However, few renowned schools pursued him for their Division I football teams. Brady had to be proactive if he wanted to keep playing football in college. So, with the assistance of his father (and at the cost of about $2,000), Brady compiled a videotape of highlights from his two years as a varsity QB at Junipero Serra and sent them unsolicited to more than 50 college athletic departments.

At the behest of his parents, those videos went primarily to schools that were academically rigorous, should Brady's football career end at the college level—that way he'd have a stellar education to prepare him for burgeoning adulthood. After all that solicitation, fewer than ten schools showed any interest in Brady. The short list included the University of Illinois, the University of Michigan, UCLA, USC, and UC Berkeley, located about 40 miles from his hometown of San Mateo.

While Brady would've preferred playing closer to home, he decided to attend the University of Michigan. Bill Harris, an assistant coach at Michigan, saw some promise in Brady, but he asked for more game footage, wanting to see video of his best *and* worst moments to get a sense of Brady's overall style. He liked what he saw, arranged a campus visit, and urged Michigan to make an offer. In 1995, Brady enrolled and moved to the University of Michigan.

LIFE LESSONS FROM A LEGEND

- ALLOW YOUR VALUES TO BOLSTER AND INSPIRE YOU.
- FOLLOW YOUR OWN VISION. NO ONE ELSE'S MATTERS.
- BE AS PATIENT AS YOU ARE PASSIONATE.
- THERE'S ALWAYS ROOM FOR IMPROVEMENT.

KNOW YOUR WORTH

At every level of Tom Brady's rise to football phenom, he faced conjecture that the sport just wasn't for him—that he ought to just quit and find another passion or pursuit. In 2000, an NFL scout called Brady "awful" and "weak," while a quarterback coach lamented that he had "the size but not enough arm," and a general manager wrote of the QB, "Just wish he was a better athlete." But Brady persisted, never failing to put in the effort to make himself better, undeniably so, developing the skills and even changing his body into that of an elite athlete.

He was always willing to put in the time and work to make himself the best football player he could be. He was smart enough to know that he needed to change himself and adapt to the game he loved in order to succeed in it. The thrill for him was seeing how much better he could get as a player, and to be able to measure that improvement:

> *"I think the great part about what I do is that there's a scoreboard. At the end of every week, you*

know how you did. You know how well you prepared. You know whether you executed your game plan. There's a tangible score."

UTILIZE THE WAITING PERIODS

The University of Michigan coaches might have seemed the most enthusiastic about Brady's talent, but when he arrived at the school ready to play in the fall of 1995, he did not receive the warm welcome he expected. The incoming freshman ranked No. 7 on the Michigan Wolverines' depth chart. That meant he wasn't just a backup; he was the backup to the backup to the backup to the backup to the backup to the backup to the team's starting quarterback. As his father, Tom Brady Sr., put it, "I guess there were more highly recruited prospects, but Tommy never had any doubt about his abilities."

Brady wouldn't even enjoy one second of playing time that freshman season at Michigan. He was "redshirted," meaning he was allowed to practice and develop his skills with the team, but he wasn't allowed to play. Brady didn't get discouraged. He used his benching as an opportunity. There was no pressure on him to perform—all he had to do was practice with and scrimmage against his elite football teammates. And so, while he didn't see any action on the field, he was able to continue to get better and better.

Brady's second season at the University of Michigan, and his first as an eligible player, was uneventful. Low on the depth chart behind starter Scott Dreisbach and promising second-stringer Brian Griese, Brady threw a grand total of three completions in five attempted

"I'VE ALWAYS BEEN THE UNDERDOG."

"I WAS THE KID THAT WAS THE 199TH PICK THAT NEVER HAD THE BODY FOR IT."

passes in the 1996 season, appearing in just two games, all in late-game "garbage time," when the outcome has been all but assured and the teams are just running out the clock. In the very first play of his first game, Brady reared back, threw the ball, then suffered a hit from a UCLA lineman. The pass went off course, was intercepted, and returned by UCLA for a touchdown; Michigan lost in a blowout, 38-9. The other game in which Brady played was an uneventful 44-10 rout of Minnesota. It didn't look like Brady, forever having to prove himself, would have much luck or success at the college level. And yet, he persisted, striving to make himself undeniable. Undaunted by the lack of playing time, he spent the offseason working out hard.

WORK AS HARD AS YOU NEED TO (AND THEN SOME)

During the 1997 season, Brady's second as a college player, Michigan's offense was led by starting quarterback Brian Griese, a full-on star who'd worked his way out of the

GAME ON

Tom Brady is hypercompetitive, even with his friends and colleagues. While hanging out with Patriots teammates, he once broke a table tennis paddle during a heated game, threw a backgammon board across a room, and felt his way down a cliff to retrieve an errant golf ball so he wouldn't have to accept a penalty stroke.

"YOU DON'T NEED TO BE THE 'NEXT' ANYBODY. YOU JUST NEED TO BE THE BEST VERSION OF YOU."

shadow of Scott Dreisbach. Griese played so well that Brady had little to no shot of ever seeing much on-field time for the Wolverines. In the 1997 season, Brady threw a mere 15 passes; meanwhile, Griese directed Michigan to an undefeated season, a national championship, and won the most valuable player award in the 1998 Rose Bowl. All Brady could do was study his team's playbooks, observe Griese, work out with his teammates, and develop his skills. Despite the lack of opportunity to show it, Brady knew that he had a lot of talent, and that he had to just wait for his moment. Quitting was not an option.

Brady's teammates noticed and appreciated his efforts. Upon meeting Brady, Griese thought the future star was "laid back." He soon learned that he was wrong. He was methodical and relentless. "There was nobody who was going to outwork him," Griese said in 2018. Brady spent hours watching film of games he didn't even play in and dissecting plays and delivering reports to his teammates on bus rides home from games. He was more like an unofficial coach or consultant, developing the mental tools necessary for football success and sharing them with the other players.

His tenacity and willingness to help out the team in whatever way he could meant coaches were willing to take a chance on Brady. In the fall of 1998, his third season as an eligible player, Brady had finally outlasted and outmaneuvered everybody else

"I FIND THAT PEOPLE WHO ARE BLESSED WITH THE MOST TALENT DON'T EVER DEVELOP THAT ATTITUDE, AND THE ONES WHO AREN'T BLESSED IN THAT WAY ARE THE MOST COMPETITIVE AND HAVE THE BIGGEST HEART."

"I THINK SOMETIMES IN LIFE THE BIGGEST CHALLENGES END UP BEING THE BEST THINGS THAT HAPPEN."

on the depth chart. With Griese graduating, Brady landed the gig of starting quarterback for the Michigan Wolverines. No longer held back from showing his capabilities, Brady rose to the occasion and took the Wolverines to a 10-1 record, setting new Michigan benchmarks for pass attempts and completions. He quickly became one of the top college quarterbacks in the nation.

PROVE YOURSELF UNDER PRESSURE

It seemed as though Brady's persistence had paid off, but he still had one more hurdle to face in his collegiate career. During Brady's senior campaign, coach Lloyd Carr added rookie Drew Henson to the roster. Carr would alternate between Brady and Henson in the first halves of games, and whoever did better would get to play QB in the second half. Brady was up to the challenge— being forced to fight for his job made him push himself harder than ever. For the first five games of the season, Brady studied the film of his performance nightly, bent on improvement. He was able to apply what he learned going forward, and he used it to stand out in the sixth game of the season, when he led

"I THOUGHT I WOULD NEVER GET A CHANCE TO PLAY, UNTIL ONE TIME I DID, BECAUSE I WAS PREPARED AND THE OPPORTUNITY PRESENTED ITSELF."

Michigan from a 17-point deficit with 18 minutes to go, throwing for 241 yards. From that point on, he was Michigan's one and only leading quarterback. He orchestrated come-from-behind victories against Notre Dame, Indiana, and Penn State. Against Alabama in the prestigious Orange Bowl, Brady took charge in an overtime thriller that Michigan won by a single point.

YOU ONLY NEED ONE SHOT

Though he proved his physical and mental football mettle at the University of Michigan and in an Orange Bowl performance in which he set records for passing yards (369) and touchdowns (four), the NFL wasn't really interested in Tom Brady. According to a pre-2000 NFL Draft scouting report, experts pegged Brady as too skinny and too slight in size to hold his own against opposing hulking linebackers and defensive ends. Scouts thought Brady lacked strength, mobility, a powerful arm, and commented that he couldn't throw a football in a tight spiral pattern, a basic quarterback ability. Their concerns were validated at the NFL Draft Combine, where prospects show off their skills in timed and measured tests. Brady ran the 40-yard dash in 5.24 seconds, the second slowest among all quarterbacks. His 24.5-inch vertical leap was also among the worst among his position. Draft experts estimated that if he was drafted at all, Brady would fall somewhere between picks 150 and 200. NFL Draft expert Mel Kiper Jr. rated 576 quarterbacks that year, and Brady ranked dead last.

Only one NFL executive contacted Michigan's Lloyd Carr about Tom Brady: New England Patriots vice president of player personnel Bobby

LEAVE IT ALL ON THE FIELD

After the Orange Bowl, Tom Brady was so sore that he could barely walk. His father had to carry his equipment bag for him.

"TO ME, WHAT SEPARATES REALLY GOOD PLAYERS FROM GREAT PLAYERS: EXECUTE WELL UNDER PRESSURE."

"THEY CAN'T MEASURE HEART. WHETHER YOU'RE PICKED FIRST, LAST, OR NOT AT ALL, YOU DECIDE WHAT HAPPENS NEXT, EVERY DAY."

Grier. He looked past Brady's poor showing at the NFL Draft Combine and saw promise in the player's intelligence, mental toughness, and leadership qualities—qualities that could help the Pats rebuild the franchise. At that time, the Patriots were historically bad. Around as part of the NFL-absorbed AFL since the early 1960s, they didn't reach a Super Bowl until 1986, losing to the Chicago Bears, 46-10. Another came in the mid-1990s, a 35-21 loss to the Green Bay Packers. They were anything but dynastic at this point. They were also over the salary cap and had to pick for need first, selecting players to fill particular gaps in the roster according to position, while Brady remained on the board. Had he not been drafted by the Patriots, Brady might not have been drafted at all.

BE READY FOR YOUR BIG MOMENT

Some of the most important and accomplished quarterbacks in football history were the No. 1 NFL Draft pick the year they entered the league, like Terry Bradshaw, Troy Aikman, John

"IF YOU DON'T BELIEVE IN YOURSELF WHY IS ANYONE ELSE GOING TO BELIEVE IN YOU?"

LOW PICK, HIGH HOPES

Most players drafted around No. 200 don't even make it to an NFL roster, and if they do, they don't last more than two years in the league. Only one quarterback drafted lower than Tom Brady has been inducted into the Pro Football Hall of Fame: Bart Starr (No. 200 in the 1956 NFL Draft).

Elway, and Drew Bledsoe. Bledsoe, taken by the New England Patriots in 1993, was the team's starting quarterback for eight seasons.

In 2000, Brady was set to be the Patriots' fourth-string QB, behind Drew Bledsoe, John Friesz, and Michael Bishop. After all, he was the 199th overall pick in the sixth round. Regardless, when he met boss Robert Kraft, he introduced himself as "the best decision" the team ever made. He completed one pass in three attempts in the one game he played in his rookie season for a grand total of six yards.

In 2001, Brady signed a 10-year, $103 million contract with the Patriots. He started off as a no-name backup on the roster, but eventually Brady leapfrogged the other quarterbacks, having added 40 pounds of muscle in the offseason to his 180-pound frame.

"YOU GUYS KNOW HOW MANY TIMES I HAVE BEEN TURNED DOWN IN MY LIFE?"

"THIS IS A PERFECT EXAMPLE OF WHAT HAPPENS WHEN GUYS BELIEVE IN EACH OTHER."

It was in the second game of his second season with the Pats that Brady would be asked to prove his worth. A rough hit cut a blood vessel in Drew Bledsoe's chest, and led to internal bleeding. Bledsoe had also sustained a concussion. His replacement: Tom Brady.

Brady came in with 2:16 on the clock in the fourth quarter and couldn't bring the team back from a 10-3 deficit. But *he played*. And he never yielded the job back. In his first start, he beat Peyton Manning's Indianapolis Colts, 44-13. A few games later, down by 10 in the fourth, he got into a tie, then won in overtime against the San Diego Chargers. Clearly, Tom Brady was a young star to watch. Proving the scouting report wrong and making his low draft position a steal, Brady threw for 2,843 yards and 18 touchdowns. The Patriots finished the season, thanks in large part to Tom Brady, with an 11-5 record. In the AFC Championship, Brady sustained a knee injury during the game, and Drew Bledsoe, the backup to his former backup, stepped in to win the game. But by then the team was Brady's. Brady started the 2002 Super Bowl against the favored St. Louis Rams. In this, the biggest game of his life at the time, Brady faced a 17-17 tie with less than two minutes left. And then clutch Brady came to life. On the final drive of the game, Brady completed five of six passes, gaining enough yardage to move into field goal range. Adam Vinatieri then made the game-winning field goal. And so, just like that, in his first full season as a starting QB, Tom Brady had become the Super Bowl's Most Valuable Player and the youngest quarterback to win a Super Bowl. To add even more weight to the moment, it was the first Super Bowl win in Patriots history. The

WAKE UP, BRADY

Tom Brady fell asleep in his team's locker room before his first Super Bowl in 2002. He woke up with just twelve minutes until game time. "I just felt good about where I was at," he explained when someone questioned how he could be so relaxed. "I just felt like I was very prepared."

franchise's destiny now lay with Brady. The team traded Bledsoe to the Buffalo Bills, and Brady became the full-time permanent starting quarterback for New England.

Winning would become a matter of course for Brady, a player who the experts didn't think had what it took to be a Super Bowl-level quarterback.

LIFE LESSONS FROM A LEGEND

- LET YOUR CONFIDENCE IN YOUR ABILITIES GUIDE YOU.
- SHORTCOMINGS AREN'T PREDICTORS OF LATER FAILURES.
- HAVE FAITH AND WORK HARD.
- UTILIZE OPPORTUNITIES WHEN THEY'RE GIVEN.
- IF YOU FAIL, KEEP TRYING. AND THEN KEEP TRYING SOME MORE.

NEVER GIVE UP

Tom Brady does not quit. Because he loves what he does, because he's singularly focused and motivated on the eventual end result, and because he believes in what he's capable of doing, he's fueled to go for it, despite any setbacks and challenges he may encounter.

BELIEVE IN YOURSELF

For many years, Brady had to believe in his abilities and bolster his own confidence when others didn't see his value. He didn't start playing football until high school, and for two years of that experience, he mainly practiced with the team. In college, he faced a similar struggle, fighting for playing time against more established members of the University of Michigan football team and an upstart challenger.

Even after proving himself a true talent at the college level, in the regular season and in widely viewed bowl games, he wasn't drafted high at all. He was picked No. 199 in the 2000 NFL Draft behind six other quarterbacks. It would have been

"TO ANYONE
[EXPERIENCING]
FEAR OF FAILURE,
YOU'RE NOT ALONE.
THE MAGIC YOU'RE
LOOKING FOR IS IN
THE WILL OF TRYING
AND NOT GIVING UP."

reasonable for Brady to complain or to give up on his dream at any of those roadblocks, but he didn't.

SETBACKS ARE PART OF THE JOURNEY

Injuries are the greatest adversity faced by elite professional athletes. It's a work hazard, so it's almost guaranteed that at some point during a long football career, a player is going to get injured. How they handle that injury, its ramifications, and how they work their way back to the top, gives a lot of insight into their character. Tom Brady has suffered only one significant injury in his two-decade stint as an NFL quarterback, a remarkably low number. It's because of his tenacity and his commitment to football that it is a forgettable blip in his long career.

The 2008 season was underway, and Tom Brady and the New England Patriots were playing a home game against the Kansas City Chiefs. Brady threw seven completions in 11 attempts for 76 yards in the first half of the first quarter, appearing to be well on the way to another legendary season with impressive statistics and a deep post-season run. But just eight minutes into the 2008 regular season, Kansas City safety Bernard Pollard nailed a ball-holding Brady just below the knees. He crumbled to the ground, seriously hurt for the first time. He needed help from team doctors to walk off the field. Post-game tests revealed a torn anterior cruciate ligament (ACL) and a torn medial collateral ligament (MCL) in his left knee.

Medical staff had to wait about a month for the MCL to heal before they could treat the ACL. This kind of injury, in which vital muscles are completely torn, can take a year for a full recovery. Brady would miss the rest of the 2008–NFL season.

STAT ⚡ Through the 2021–22 season, Tom Brady staged 42 fourth-quarter comebacks, the second-most in NFL history.

"YOU HAVE TO TAKE THE GOOD WITH THE BAD."

He had to face that hard truth, while the Patriots had to prepare his replacement. Backup quarterback Matt Cassel rose to the occasion.

CONTRIBUTE IN ANY WAY YOU CAN

Just because he couldn't play football (or walk all that well) didn't mean that Tom Brady wasn't dedicated to his craft, his sport, and his team. He still considered himself a part of the Patriots' 2008 campaign, so he took it upon himself to contribute however he could. Just a few days after his surgery, he became a regular presence at the Patriots' practice facility, cheering on his teammates and encouraging them to play harder. He reviewed videos of their games and pointed out areas of improvement. The coaches had asked him not to hang out on the sidelines during games, determining that his

TAKE A KNEE

During the 2008 season when he was sidelined with a knee injury, Tom Brady proposed to his then-girlfriend Gisele Bündchen. He insisted on doing it the traditional way, down on one knee, despite the tremendous pain and his recent recovery from three consecutive staph infections.

"I HAD A
CONFIDENCE
IN ME. . . .
I ALWAYS SAID
'MAN, IF THEY PUT
ME ON THE FIELD,
THEY'RE NEVER GOING
TO TAKE ME OFF.'"

"I THINK WE INSTILLED FEAR IN OTHER TEAMS BECAUSE WE WERE ALL GOING TO COMPETE TO BE THE BEST WE COULD BE ON THAT FIELD EVERY SINGLE GAME."

presence would be distracting and earn too much attention from the media and players on both sides. So Brady did all of his unofficial coaching and cheerleading of his fellow Patriots in private.

Brady turned his slow rehabilitation into a teachable moment. His teammates got to see his progress while witnessing all the work he was putting into his recovery. It kept them motivated and gave them perspective on how fortunate they were to be healthy enough to play and to enjoy the benefit of being trained and guided by one of the best players in the league. Brady even worked with backup Matt Cassel, offering insights, advice, and on-field experience working within the Patriots' offensive system. Cassel led the Patriots to an 11-5 record, including five wins in the final six

"THINGS DON'T CORRECT THEMSELVES. YOU'VE GOT TO GO OUT THERE AND WORK HARD TO CORRECT THEM."

"TO ME, FOOTBALL IS SO MUCH ABOUT MENTAL TOUGHNESS, IT'S DIGGING DEEP, IT'S DOING WHATEVER YOU NEED TO DO TO HELP A TEAM WIN AND THAT COMES IN A LOT OF SHAPES AND FORMS."

games. But because other teams did just a little bit better than they did, the Patriots didn't win the AFC East, and they didn't make the playoffs.

It was almost unheard of for a team with a record that stellar *not* to move on to the postseason. They had, however, grown as a team and managed new challenges. They had seen firsthand that they could raise individual levels of play and collectively succeed.

Tom Brady returned for the 2009 season ready to contribute all he had. He was just as good, if not better, than he was before the injury, and he was not about to let a temporary setback be anything more than temporary.

ACT LIKE YOU'VE GOT SOMETHING TO PROVE

In the first game of the 2009 season, Brady completed nearly 75 percent of his passes. After struggling in the first half, he showed glimpses of classic, clutch Brady, leading two touchdown drives in the final two minutes of the game to eke out a

25-24 win over the Buffalo Bills. But the Patriots had an overall middling start to the season, at 3-2. Fans and pundits alike wondered if Brady was on the decline, either due to age (he was nearing a decade in the league) or due to his leg injuries. Brady kept his focus and silenced the critics. In a game against the Tennessee Titans, he completed 85 percent of his passes for 380 yards and six touchdowns (five in the final ten minutes of the second quarter). Final score: New England 59, Tennessee 0.

He surpassed his top season, reaching a personal record of 4,398 yards, 28 touchdowns, and a 96.2 rating. He was subsequently honored for his efforts by winning the NFL Comeback Player of the Year Award. It came as a surprise, then, when the Pats were eliminated in the first round of the playoffs, losing 33-14 to the Baltimore Ravens. Brady played one of the worst games of his career, throwing for 154 yards with two touchdowns, three interceptions, and a fumble on the first drive, and he'd have to

"YOU PUSH YOUR BODY TO THE LIMITS, BUT YOU HAVE TO TRAIN YOUR BODY TO DEAL WITH THE LIMITS."

spend the entire offseason analyzing and learning from his mistakes. That poor playoff performance only fueled his fire to succeed.

In the 2010 season, Tom Brady seemed like a man on a mission to prove that he wasn't too old to play well and wasn't diminished by his injury. After a messy loss to the New York Jets to start the season, or maybe because of it, Brady went on a 13-1 streak and finished with a 14-2 record, his best since the Patriots went undefeated in 2007. In the divisional round of the playoffs against the Jets, Brady threw 29 for 45 and 299 yards, but the Jets outmaneuvered the Patriots throughout the game. Never one to give up, he attempted a signature Brady comeback late in the fourth quarter with a fast drive that ended with a long and

STAT ⚡ Under Tom Brady, the New England Patriots won 17 division titles in 19 seasons. The team also made it to 13 AFC Championship games, including eight straight.

"MENTALLY, THE ONLY PLAYERS WHO SURVIVE IN THE PROS ARE THE ONES ABLE TO MANAGE ALL THEIR RESPONSIBILITIES. EVERYBODY STRUGGLES IN DIFFERENT WAYS."

successful field goal, and then another one-minute drive with a 13-yard touchdown pass to Deion Branch. But the Jets pulled it out.

Once more, Brady had to keep his cool, lay in wait, and show everyone that he'd come back harder and stronger next year with more to prove. And he did, inching back to unmatched glory with a 13-3 record and a berth in the Super Bowl in February 2012. Facing the New

York Giants, Brady's Patriots fell behind 9-0, only to rally hard in the third quarter to gain a 17-9 lead, thanks to a 21-yard touchdown pass and a 79-yard touchdown drive from Brady. The Giants wound up winning the game, 21-17, but Brady had made a statement.

JUST KEEP GOING

Even deep into his illustrious career, Tom Brady would be faced with circumstances so challenging and odds stacked so clearly against him that most other quarterbacks would relent.

The 2016–17 NFL season began and played out as a truly dark and challenging chapter in Brady's adult life, personally and professionally. His abilities, faith, character, and calm were all tested in great measure. In January 2015, Tom Brady and the New England Patriots easily defeated the Indianapolis Colts 45-7 in the AFC Championship game. But during the game, officials replaced the 12 game balls with backups, and in the coming days, the NFL would launch an investigation into whether the Patriots purposely deflated balls in order to make them easier to throw. The balls were tested and found to be under the league minimum inflation level of 12.5 pounds per square inch. Inherent in all of this was the implication that Brady was cheating, that everything he'd accomplished wasn't really all that impressive or legitimate because he'd broken the rules to get to where he was. Brady called the accusations "ridiculous." He denied being involved in altering the game balls.

A report found evidence that Patriots equipment managers John Jastremski and Jim McNally had likely orchestrated the ball-deflation scheme, sneaking balls away from a holding area to deflate them with

"I DON'T NEED TO DEFEND MYSELF."

"AT THE END OF THE DAY, IT'S ONLY US. AND WE'RE ONLY RESPONSIBLE TO MAKE OURSELVES HAPPY."

"I ALWAYS KIND OF ADHERE TO, 'IF YOU'RE EXPLAINING, YOU'RE LOSING.'"

a needle in a bathroom. Brady was linked because he held multiple conversations with Jastremski, and later destroyed his phone, something he said he regularly did. NFL commissioner Roger Goodell called Brady's destruction an obstruction of justice.

In May 2015, the NFL suspended Brady for four games and fined the Patriots $1 million. Brady appealed his suspension with the NFL Players Association. A judge overturned the NFL's suspension, which allowed Brady to play in 2015. Then the Second Circuit Court of Appeals heard the case in 2016, and two of the judges on the three-judge panel reinstated the suspension. After 10 hours of testimony, the suspension wasn't reduced. He'd serve that suspension, the first and—to date— last of his career, at the beginning of the 2016 season.

Brady was more than ready to put the whole scandal behind him:

"I defended myself for a long time. I said what I had to say multiple times in front of a lot of different people—in court, in public."

REDIRECT THE NEGATIVE ENERGY

Brady could have appealed the suspension again and pushed the case to the Supreme Court, but he knew when he was beaten, so he chose instead to focus his energy on his game. It was, for him, a difficult exercise in acceptance:

"You've got to know when to fight, and you've got to ultimately know when it's taking too much out of you to fight. And I realized that I wasn't going to win. It's hard to beat 31 billionaires in court. And I thought we gave it a great fight, but in the end, you know, just dealing with the results of what the New York circuit judge decided, I decided to put that behind me and then move on to the next year."

He harnessed his anger and frustration and turned it into something positive: motivation and inspiration. After Brady waited

"I WANTED TO GO REPRESENT WHAT I WAS ALL ABOUT. AND THE WAY I COULD DO THAT WAS ON THE FOOTBALL FIELD."

"YOU CAN'T GO OUT AND PRACTICE AVERAGE ON WEDNESDAY, AVERAGE ON THURSDAY, OKAY ON FRIDAY, AND THEN EXPECT TO PLAY WELL ON SUNDAY."

out his four-game suspension, the Patriots went on a tear, going 11-1, with Brady throwing 28 touchdowns and only two interceptions during that span.

Privately, he was also dealing with a sensitive personal issue. His mother, Galynn, was in the midst of chemotherapy treatment for cancer. She had always been in the stands watching many of her son's games, but she was noticeably absent during the 2016–17 season. Her struggle,

and the fear of losing his mom, took a toll on Brady and his entire family, a very close-knit bunch. Fortunately, Galynn made it through treatment, and she was well enough to attend that year's Super Bowl.

In the 2017 Super Bowl, Brady's New England Patriots trailed the Atlanta Falcons by a lopsided score of 28-3 heading into the fourth quarter. But Brady rallied, leading the biggest Super Bowl comeback in history. His multiple touchdown passes

"GOTTA PLAY TOUGHER. GOTTA PLAY HARDER. HARDER, TOUGHER, EVERYTHING. EVERYTHING WE'VE GOT."

resulted in a 28-28 tie at the end of regulation, forcing an overtime period in which Brady's team proved victorious with a final score of 34-28. Brady just didn't—or couldn't—give up. Brady was overheard on the sidelines at the 2017 Super Bowl, just before the Patriots' come-from-behind victory drive, urging his team to play harder.

LIFE LESSONS FROM A LEGEND

-  **TRUST YOUR GUT, BELIEVE IN YOUR OWN ABILITIES, AND FOLLOW YOUR PLAN.**

- **ENSURE THAT SETBACKS ARE ONLY TEMPORARY SETBACKS.**

- **WHEN YOU'RE SIDELINED, PUT YOURSELF BACK INTO THE GAME IN ANY WAY POSSIBLE.**

- **STAY HUNGRY AND ALWAYS PLAY LIKE THE UNDERDOG.**

- **KEEP CALM AND DEFLECT NEGATIVITY.**

- **ACCEPT WHAT YOU CAN'T CONTROL.**

FORM A TEAM AND LEAD IT

Very few accomplishments are made in a vacuum or by oneself. Life is a team sport, and as such, it takes a whole community of support to help any one person meet their goals, especially when those goals are lofty.

Tom Brady has one goal each season, and it's the same goal he's had every season for more than 20 years: to win the Super Bowl in February. He works backward from there, months in advance, training—not just for himself—but to create the team that's going to get him there. Even as the star quarterback, he's still just one part of the plan, a cog in a massive system of players who have to trust each other to win games.

Football is a widely collaborative endeavor across a massive team. The average NFL team features 53 active roster members, with at least a dozen more on the practice squad, and all of them are highly specialized in a defensive or offensive position. Then there are coaches, scouts, owners, nutritionists, and front-office and other on-field personnel. An NFL team can only be successful if everyone involved is working from the same point of view with the same goals in mind.

It's up to the coach—and the on-field leader, the team's quarterback—to execute that plan with every action. Tom Brady led the New England Patriots to six Super Bowl wins (and a seventh with the Tampa Bay Buccaneers) because he knows how to lead

"YOU PUT ALL THE OTHER STUFF ASIDE AND GO OUT AND DO YOUR JOB, AND MINE IS TO BE THE BEST I CAN BE FOR MY TEAMMATES."

"WHEN YOU'RE ONE OF THE LEADERS OF THE TEAM, THERE ARE NO DAYS OFF."

"IF YOU'RE A QUARTERBACK, YOU WANT EVERYTHING ON YOUR SHOULDERS. YOU WANT TO BE THE ONE TO MAKE THE DECISIONS."

and manage a team. When Brady played QB in New England, the team's mantra was "do your job." Everybody knew their role, and they were appreciated and respected for it.

FIND SUPPORT WHEN YOU NEED IT

One solid strategy for getting good at something is to learn from experts in your field. Tom Brady found his football mentors long before he ever even took a snap in an organized football game. As a kid looking to get onto his high school teams, he frequently attended youth football camps near his home at the College of San Mateo. From the moment he knew he wanted to be a quarterback, he set out to learn the basics and mechanics of throwing from one of

---

STAT ⚡ Tom Brady's average win-loss regular season record as a starting quarterback was 12 wins and 4 losses.

---

the camp operators. He lucked out and paid attention, because that throwing coach was Tony Graziani, a former NFL quarterback and Arena Football League star. With his openness to learning and pros to guide him, there would be no holding Brady back.

Brady's support team includes mentors and coaches who helped frame his understanding of his role on the team (whether he was injured or benched or starting) and taught him how to manage the frustration inherent in his line of work. When he was way down on

"MY JOB IS TO PLAY QUARTERBACK AND I'M GOING TO DO THAT THE BEST WAY I KNOW HOW BECAUSE I OWE THAT TO MY TEAMMATES."

"I LOVE BEING PART OF A TEAM; I LOVE WORKING TOWARD A COMMON GOAL."

the depth chart at the University of Michigan, Brady's lack of playing time caused him major anxiety and frustration. The pressure of his own expectations and of living in his sisters' shadows paired with his ceaseless competitive fire left him distraught. After considering transferring from Michigan to UC Berkeley (just down the road from his hometown of San Mateo), Brady turned to new support staff and decided to stick it out. He hired a sports psychologist to help him get over his mental blocks. He began to visualize his goals and craft a step-by-step process to achieve them. He stopped worrying about how others played and focused on his own performance, releasing

TREAT PEOPLE RIGHT

Whenever a new player joins his team, regardless of their accolades, Brady makes a point to introduce himself and welcome them. He takes the time to learn their name and familiarize himself with their history and stats.

"YOU EARN THE TRUST AND RESPECT OF THOSE AROUND THROUGH YOUR COMMITMENT EVERY SINGLE DAY."

"THE TOUGHEST
TIMES ALWAYS
TAUGHT ME
THE MOST
IMPORTANT
LESSONS."

his tendency to try and control everything about the game. Then, in working with Michigan assistant Greg Harden, he took his psychologist's advice and stopped focusing on what he wasn't doing. He began to approach his sport like a craft instead of a game of winners and losers. He used the opportunity that this gap in his playing time allowed him to strengthen his mental game. Both new "team" members helped Brady build his confidence, especially Harden, who he says helped him work his way to his first major football accomplishment, guiding the Wolverines to a Citrus Bowl victory. He later used his new confidence and team-first mindset to go on a winning streak in college, and later brought it with him to his NFL teams.

A FAMILY IS A TEAM AND A TEAM IS A FAMILY

There's a sense of solidarity that comes with a team mentality of "us against them," whether it's family or teammates together in the huddle. During the "Deflategate"

scandal, as it became known, when the Patriots (and Brady specifically) were accused of secretly and illegally letting the air out of game balls to make them allegedly easier to throw, Brady refused to speak to the media about it and never admitted any wrongdoing. Instead, he relied heavily on his inner circle for support. Gisele Bündchen, his wife at the time, was the core of it:

"I'm a lucky man. I've been very blessed with support from my family and certainly her, and there's no bigger supporter that I have than her and vice versa. I've been very blessed to have an incredible relationship with my life partner."

He explained what it meant to have Gisele in his corner: "She helped me up when I was weak and angry and sad and depressed. That was," he confirmed, "a really dark time." Despite problems that later emerged in their marriage, Gisele bolstered Brady through many personal and professional storms.

Brady is the kind of player who puts his team first. Although he was the most dominant and victorious quarterback of the 21st century, only briefly did he get paid like it. In August 2002, he signed a five-year, $30.5 million contract, with bonuses for every conference championship and Super Bowl won. In 2005, he negotiated a new contract, six years for $60 million. In 2010, that changed to a four-year, $72 million deal. Only with that extension, and after three Super Bowl victories, was Brady the highest-paid quarterback in the NFL. (Within two years, Peyton Manning would sign a contract worth more than Brady's.) That is by design and by choice. Brady constantly restructured his contract to help ensure that the Patriots organization had plenty of money left over to recruit and sign top-notch free agents. He did the same with the Tampa Bay Buccaneers. Just before the 2022

NFL Draft and free-agent signing season, Brady agreed to restructure his contract and take a little less money, which gave the team an extra $6 million to use to lure top recruits. Brady knows he needs to turn down some money in order to bring the best colleagues possible to his team. He's always been more about the winning than the money, which, for Brady, is more than enough to live on anyway.

CREATE NEW TEAMS WHEN NECESSARY

Despite his history and commitment to the New England Patriots, when Tom Brady perceived that the tight, team-minded atmosphere was slipping, he knew that it was time to move on. Over the age of 40 and still considered among the league's most elite players, Brady wanted a long-term contract with the Patriots. The team's executives were unwilling

STAT ⚡ Tom Brady has played in about one-fifth of all the Super Bowls ever played.

"THE BETTER YOU ARE, THE BETTER YOU WANT TO BE AROUND PEOPLE WHO ARE EQUALLY TALENTED."

to offer it, fearing Brady would soon retire. They didn't see eye to eye, and Brady felt disrespected, so much so that he was willing to move to a new atmosphere and find his way with a new team, albeit one with the same goals he'd always had: win games and then win the Super Bowl.

When Brady signed a deal with the Tampa Bay Buccaneers, it was a $50 million, two-year contract.

It was the largest contract Brady had ever signed in terms of annual salary, but it still didn't place him among the top 10 highest-earning quarterbacks in the NFL at the time. It did, however, leave the team with more signing money (especially after he restructured the contract to create more salary cap space). Brady's flexibility allowed the Bucs to recruit top players—and those players helped Brady and the rest of the team reach and win the Super

"IF YOU'RE LUCKY,
YOU'LL HAVE FAMILY,
TEAMMATES, COACHES,
AND TRAINERS
ALONG THE WAY
WHO WILL HELP YOU
WHEN YOU LOSE
FAITH IN YOURSELF."

Bowl in the quarterback's first year in Florida. One of those players was Brady's frequent Patriots target, Rob Gronkowski. Brady personally insisted the Bucs maneuver to trade for his old teammate—because he was an integral member of Brady's personal winning squad.

WORK WELL WITH OTHERS

Brady's ability to stay in perfect step with his coach and carry out the coach's vision has been key to his athletic achievements. A football team's head coach, particularly a thoughtful, immensely calculating one like longtime Patriots leader Bill Belichick, is the true squad leader, responsible for giving everyone a job to do. It's the job of the quarterback to be the on-field version of the coach, executing orders and ensuring that everybody does their job correctly. Brady is a prodigy in that regard, working successfully with Belichick (they both joined the Patriots in 2000) and other Patriots coaches to ensure that all their pregame plans, meticulously researched, reviewed, and practiced, would be carried out in the game

itself. This fine-tuned relationship helped Brady and Belichick win six Super Bowls.

ENCOURAGE OTHERS' SUCCESSES

When Brady abruptly switched to the Tampa Bay Buccaneers in 2020, despite being the new guy, he immediately set about creating a cohesive and supportive team framework. Before the season began, Brady reportedly contacted every member of the Tampa Bay roster and helped them plan their offseason training regimen. Head coach Bruce Arians credited Brady with singlehandedly convincing the team that a Super Bowl run (or victory) was something they could feasibly achieve. The year before Brady's arrival, they'd finished a mediocre 7-9. With Brady, they improved to 11-5 and won their first Super Bowl in nearly two decades. "The belief he gave to this organization that it could be done. It only took one man," Arians said. Brady had spent a season proving his leadership skills and building trust, which included sending frequent, encouraging text messages to members of his team. His efforts had a positive effect. "Little things like that go a long way," Patriots wide receiver Julian Edelman remarked. "It made me want to go out and play hard for him because he's the G.O.A.T."

LIFE LESSONS FROM A LEGEND

- SEEK OUT ADVICE, WISDOM, AND SUPPORT FROM THOSE WHO CARE.

- TREAT A TEAM LIKE A FAMILY, WITH LOVE, RESPECT, AND LOYALTY.

- BE FLEXIBLE AND UNAFRAID OF CHANGE.

- LET YOUR ACTIONS REFLECT YOUR VALUES.

- BE THE LEADER YOUR TEAM NEEDS.

STAY HUMBLE; STAY SMART

A winning mindset requires a combination of just the right amounts of confidence and humility. Confidence pushes you forward, convinced that you are capable of whatever challenge lies ahead. But humility is equally important. Having a realistic self-assessment and measured outlook gives a person patience with themselves as they work toward a goal, and then gratitude—particularly to others who helped—when those goals are met.

Tom Brady has always been confident in his abilities as a football player and athletic leader, even back before he'd achieved great things. He knew that if he had half the chance, he'd show the world what he was made of and what he could accomplish. On the other hand, Brady has remained notably and observably humble, despite accomplishing more on the football field than any other player in

"WHEN YOU LOSE, TALK LITTLE. WHEN YOU WIN, TALK LESS."

history (and building an admirable off-the-turf life). An April 19, 2018, Instagram post expresses just how lucky he feels to have made it so far in life:

"One day, you will look back on your life and appreciate the struggle and have nothing but gratitude for everything that happened along the way."

Teammates who have played alongside Brady are surprised at how grounded he is despite his accomplishments. James Harrison, who played briefly for the Patriots in 2017, expected a certain amount of arrogance from the star quarterback when he first met him. He was shocked to find just the opposite, that Brady was unassuming and treated everyone around him with respect: "He's a good dude. From the practice squad guy that comes in the first day, he's like, 'Hey, how you doing? I'm Tom Brady.'" Just because he's at the top of his game doesn't mean Brady treats others like they're beneath him, and doesn't stop him from continuing to put in the work. "Brady understands that no matter who you are, the game of football doesn't owe you

BIG YEARS

In 2021, *Sports Illustrated* named Tom Brady its Sportsperson of the Year. He was only the third person to win it more than once (after Tiger Woods and LeBron James), having first received the honor in 2005 after winning his third Super Bowl.

"IF YOU HAVE
PERSPECTIVE,
IN THE END,
NOTHING BAD REALLY
EVER HAPPENS."

"NO ONE'S GOING TO HAND YOU ANYTHING."

anything," said former teammate Marcellus Wiley. Brady is less focused on what he's owed and more focused on paying forward what he's been given. Leading and teaching others is something he revels in. "I think I got to the point in my career," Brady said in 2022, "where people listen to me in different ways. So, I try to impart my wisdom and hopefully allow them to reach their potential."

DON'T REST ON YOUR LAURELS

Brady is a multimillionaire who grew up in a well-to-do family from the affluent San Francisco suburb of San Mateo. He's been voted "Man of the Year" by *GQ*, "Sexiest Athlete Alive" by *Business Insider,* and one of the "Sexiest Men Alive" by *People Magazine.* He's also married to a supermodel, and is the proud father of three healthy children. Brady knows he's got it good, and he appreciates what he has. He's a golden boy who's been tagged as the greatest football player of all time, but he bristles at being called the G.O.A.T.:

"It makes me cringe. I guess I take compliments worse. I wish you would say, 'You're trash, you're too old, you're too slow, you can't get it done no more.' And I'll say, 'Thank you very much; I'll prove you wrong.'"

He's happier being critiqued and pushed toward improvement than being coddled with praise. Brady doesn't have a sense of entitlement. He doesn't rest on his achievements or his current status, and the cutthroat world of professional sports wouldn't let him anyway. Some part of him enjoyed having to prove himself as a high school player, in college,

---

STAT ⚡ When 45-year-old Tom Brady took the field for the 2022–23 NFL season, he was the oldest player in the league. The second-oldest starting quarterback: 38-year-old Aaron Rodgers.

as worthy of the pros, and in Tampa Bay, as a 40-something quarterback supposedly past his prime. He rose to meet the challenge every time.

AIM HIGH, BUT PLAN FOR CONTINGENCIES

Not particularly gifted and not widely scouted or heralded as a high school quarterback, Tom Brady's monumental successes as a football player were far from preordained or guaranteed. He was benched for half of his high school seasons, but after demonstrating his gifts and skills over and over again, he became a backup at the University of Michigan, then worked his way to a humbling No. 199 draft selection in 2000. While it was certainly tough to sit idly by, Brady waited, hopeful enough to believe that he'd get his chance, and prepared and trained enough to know that he'd be able to execute when that opportunity arrived.

Humility helped Brady come to terms with the fact that he needed a professional backup plan in case his NFL dreams didn't happen. He didn't even consider colleges that weren't academically intensive. At the University of Michigan, Brady double majored in psychology and business administration. He graduated with a solid grade point average of 3.3, and was ready to take on internships and entry-level jobs along with his fellow classmates. While Brady crushed it on the field in the fall, he spent his summer interning at the bottom rung of the Ann Arbor, Michigan, branch of the Merrill Lynch stock brokerage. He was promoted to assistant to a senior sales broker the second summer he worked as an intern. A second path was already opening up for him.

Never one to limit himself, Brady also spent part of those summers working as a sales representative for two golf courses in Michigan and managing construction and security for the Top of the Park summer festival. But, luckily for his fans, he didn't have to pursue a career in business for long because football would soon make him a household name.

"STAY HUNGRY,
STAY HUMBLE."

"I'm really a product of what I've been around, who I was coached by, what I played against, in the era I played in. I really believe if a lot of people were in my shoes, they could accomplish the same kinds of things. So I've been very fortunate."

RESPECT YOUR COHORTS

Tom Brady is the leader of whatever team he's on by virtue of being the starting quarterback, a superstar, a veteran, and an astute student of the game. Still, he recognizes that there's a limit to everyone's expertise.

Not only does he play well within a team framework and recognize and appreciate the accomplishments of others, but he allows himself to be coached, approaching football (and his superiors) with an open mind and a willingness to learn.

Part of the reason why Brady is a G.O.A.T. is because he's constantly improving and tweaking his game. Brady works to improve his craft, and that means consulting with coaches and working with them to develop playbooks and game plans.

"INDIVIDUAL AWARDS IN A TEAM SPORT ALWAYS MAKE ME FEEL A BIT UNEASY, BECAUSE NOTHING CAN BE ACCOMPLISHED WITHOUT THE TEAM. IT'S ALWAYS ABOUT THE TEAM."

He isn't too proud to allow experts with more or different experience to inform his perspective. The unfailing respect that he shows his teammates, trusting that they have their own wisdom and contributions to the game, builds camaraderie and allows everyone to help each other strive as a whole.

Extending that courtesy to players on opposing teams comes just as naturally to him. If there's one thing Brady isn't, it's a sore winner. He is deeply driven and is highly competitive, but once he wins, he is as thoughtful and reflective as he is appreciative. For example, after defeating the Kansas City Chiefs in the 2021 Super Bowl, Brady and Patrick Mahomes, the Chiefs' young superstar quarterback, sought each other out during the postgame festivities. Brady didn't make a show of it for the media, approaching Mahomes discreetly. He wanted to show some appreciation for the competition and express his goodwill. Mahomes praised Brady for his "awesome" performance, while Brady implored the younger quarterback to "keep in touch."

STEP OUTSIDE YOUR COMFORT ZONE

Emboldened by his success on the football field and the fearless attitude that drives him, Brady doesn't shrink away from trying things outside of football. He's not afraid to dip his toes into new ventures, even at the risk of public failure.

Brady went out on a limb and tried his hand at business and entertainment ventures. He founded Brady Brand, a line of athleisure wear for men, to build on his success. The line includes tank tops, T-shirts, hooded sweatshirts, pants, and underwear that he modeled himself on his social media accounts. He also had a hand in hiring the 100-person staff of Autograph, a platform he co-founded in 2021. Autograph sells NFTs (non-fungible tokens), or digital-only art, of pop culture and sports moments. These bold investments, among others, have already brought him creative and financial success. If he hadn't ventured beyond his usual area of specialty, he could not have enjoyed the payoff.

"I'VE BEEN REALLY LUCKY THAT I'VE HAD THIS CAREER THAT I'VE LOVED TO DO FOR TWO-PLUS DECADES."

STAT ⚡ In the same season that Tom Brady's New England Patriots amassed a perfect 16-0 regular season record, he set a record-breaking 50 touchdown passes. Though it's since been broken, only three other quarterbacks—Dan Marino, Kurt Warner, and Peyton Manning—had reached 40 touchdowns in one season before Brady broke that record.

In 2003, not long after winning his first Super Bowl, Brady took a bit role in *Stuck on You,* a comedy by New England filmmaking brothers Peter and Bobby Farrelly. Knowingly playing against type, he was cast as Computer Geek #1. In 2005, Brady voiced himself in an episode of *The Simpsons* where he hires Homer Simpson to teach him how to improve his on-field celebration dance. That same year, Brady dared to become one of the few nonperformers and athletes to host NBC's sketch-comedy series *Saturday Night Live.* Breaking away from his image as serious and upstanding, Brady cut loose in a variety of sketches, including one where he quits football to open an Indian restaurant. He went on to appear in the movie adaptation of *Entourage* and a comedy called *80 for Brady.*

He even formed a content production company, 199 Productions, wryly named after his low ranking in the 2000 NFL Draft. Brady also produced two autobiographical documentary series, *Man in the Arena* and *Tom vs. Time,* as well as the Netflix series *The Greatest Roasts of All Time.*

MAKE A LONG-TERM PLAN

Before Brady announced plans to retire on February 1, 2022 at age 44, he already had a post-retirement plan in place. He knew he couldn't play football forever, but he wanted to continue to be part of the sport he has always loved. In May 2022, Brady signed a 10-year contract with

Fox Sports for $375 million. For the next stage of his career, Brady would become the lead analyst in Fox's TV coverage of NFL games.

"I feel like I can still have a great impact on the game. I could stay in the game, doing what I love to do, talking about this incredible sport."

LIFE LESSONS FROM A LEGEND

- RECOGNIZE YOUR ADVANTAGES, AND EXPRESS GRATITUDE FOR THEM.

- TREAT OTHERS WITH RESPECT.

- HAVE LOFTY GOALS AND A GOOD BACKUP PLAN.

- BE WILLING TO LEARN, EVEN WHEN YOU'RE AT THE TOP OF YOUR GAME.

- TRY NEW THINGS.

- MAKE A FUTURE PLAN THAT YOU'RE EXCITED ABOUT.

DO. YOUR. JOB.

CHAPTER 6

Tom Brady is unequivocally the most decorated man to ever play in the NFL. He's a 15-time Pro Bowl selection, a seven-time Super Bowl winner, a five-time Super Bowl MVP, a three-time regular season MVP, and a member of the league's 2000s All-Decade Team and 2010s All-Decade Team. In 2019, *USA Today* ranked Brady the No. 1 quarterback of all time (and the second-best overall player, behind only wide receiver Jerry Rice).

Because of the sheer amount of times he's entered a stadium over the course of his career, and the fact that he's consistently competing against top-tier athletes and stellar teams, Brady knows what disappointment feels like. It's just as hard to stay at the top as it is to reach the top. Even though he's football's G.O.A.T., Brady has made mistakes, experienced failure, and muddled through scandal and controversy. Where he truly showed his mettle and resilience is how he navigated those difficulties to return to greatness and the public's good graces. Brady has learned over the years that there are always going to

UNDISPUTED

Tom Brady was one of just four quarterbacks unanimously selected for the NFL 100 All-Time Team.

be elements in the game and in the industry beyond his control. All he can do is keep his eye on the prize and just keep moving forward. Brady refuses to let distractions and failures overshadow his accomplishments or weaken his drive.

EXPECT SOME HIGHS AND LOWS

Only twice since Tom Brady became a starting quarterback in the NFL, going back to the 2001–02 season, have his teams failed to win a berth in the NFL playoffs. After leading the New England Patriots to its first Super Bowl title in 2002, the following season, Brady and the Pats missed the playoffs. Then, after back-to-back Super Bowl wins in 2004 and 2005, Brady seemingly lost his winning edge. It would be a decade before the Patriots would win another Super Bowl. In that period, they missed the playoffs only once (in 2009), but repeatedly made an early exit, reaching the conference championship game just once, in 2012.

"I DIDN'T COME THIS FAR TO ONLY COME THIS FAR, SO WE'VE STILL GOT FURTHER TO GO."

"MAYBE SOME PEOPLE CAN WAKE UP AND PLAY PLAYSTATION ALL DAY, BUT THAT'S NEVER BEEN ME."

> ## "I HAVE ALWAYS BELIEVED THAT THE SPORT OF FOOTBALL IS AN 'ALL-IN' PROPOSITION. IF A 100 PERCENT COMPETITIVE COMMITMENT ISN'T THERE, YOU WON'T SUCCEED."

In the 2005 season, following two Super Bowl wins, Brady threw for 4,110 yards, 26 touchdowns, and completed 63 percent of all passes for a quarterback rating of 92.3. But these personal successes didn't translate into an impressive number of team wins or postseason glory. Brady cared most about winning another Super Bowl as a team. The Patriots went 10-6 that season, losing to the San Diego Chargers at home, 41-17, and to the Carolina Panthers, 27-17. In the AFC divisional round of the playoffs, Brady threw twice as many interceptions as he did touchdowns, and the Patriots lost to the Denver Broncos. This eliminated them from the playoffs.

TURN SETBACKS INTO OPPORTUNITIES

Sports fans don't talk about the big losses and failures in Tom Brady's professional career because they're aberrations. He didn't let them define him and neither did the world, because his successes greatly overshadowed his missteps. The few setbacks and injuries he experienced only served to highlight his winning approach to football. In December 2005, for example, Brady suffered a hernia during a game and played through it. During that offseason, as he recovered from corrective hernia surgery, Brady had more time to study his on-field mistakes and set out to try and correct them, the most proactive thing he could do at the time. He also invested that time into figuring out and helping to acquire the missing pieces of a championship team (like star linebacker Junior Seau).

The effort spent on bolstering defense paid off for the Patriots. In 2006, the team allowed 14.8 points per game, the second lowest in the NFL. The use of running backs Corey Dillon and Laurence Maroney also meant that the Pats offense moved to running the ball more as opposed to throwing, giving Brady's throwing arm a reprieve. That season, he threw for 2,529 yards and 24 touchdowns, earning the Pats a 12-4 record, a division title, and a playoff run that ended in the AFC Championship game. He lost to longtime rival Peyton Manning's Indianapolis Colts. Brady had just 232 passing yards and one touchdown, while Manning had 349 passing yards and won the game 38-34. Sometimes players have off days, but an off day for Brady was usually just a warmup for another momentous comeback.

In the 2007 NFL season, Brady managed to win his first NFL Most Valuable Player Award. He threw 50 touchdowns, a scant eight interceptions (he went ten whole games without any), and had a 69 percent completion rate. Amazingly, and for just the second time in football history, an NFL team finished the regular season undefeated: The Patriots had a 16-0 record. The only other team to do it was the Miami Dolphins in 1972, but they only had to play 14 games.

The Dolphins' undefeated season culminated in a Super Bowl win. The Patriots' undefeated season, shockingly, did not. The New York Giants, a wild card team with a 10-6 record, improbably defeated Brady and the Patriots in the Super Bowl, delivering a crushing loss. The Patriots had just 274 offensive

"I AM NOT
A PERSON THAT'S
SELF-SATISFIED JUST
BEING OUT THERE.
I WANT TO GO
OUT THERE AND
PLAY GREAT."

yards, with Brady putting up an uncharacteristically low 229 passing yards. Still, Brady had written the Patriots into the history books—even if they did go 18-1, and that one was a Super Bowl loss. The main reason they faltered: Brady got hit a lot. He was sacked five times, leaving him more and more frustrated. Other teams had figured out how to play Brady, and he'd have to adapt to the league adapting to him if he wanted to succeed. He picked himself up after every sack with a relentlessness that never waned, even when it was clear they had lost the game. After the season was over, he started training again, both body and mind.

WEATHER THE STORM

When you're as famous as Brady, a private but difficult matter becomes fodder for mass consumption and commentary. Brady experienced some issues in his personal life in 2006 and 2007 that could have embarrassed him or tainted him with scandal, but because he treated others and himself with dignity and care, he managed to rise above.

In 2004, fresh off his second Super Bowl win, Brady started dating actor Bridget Moynahan. They dated for two years and frequently appeared in public together, but decided to end their relationship in late 2006. Weeks after they announced their split, Brady began a new relationship with model Gisele Bündchen, whom he'd met while dating Moynahan but hadn't pursued romantically. After his relationship with Bündchen developed and became public knowledge, Moynahan announced that she was pregnant with Brady's baby.

WIN, LOSE, OR SHARE

When the New England Patriots lost the 2018 Super Bowl to the Philadelphia Eagles, Tom Brady's kids were so upset that their mother, Gisele Bündchen, told them that their father didn't really lose, but that he was "sharing" the win.

"[I TRY TO] NOT LOSE TOUCH WITH WHAT'S REALLY IMPORTANT, WHICH IS BEING A GOOD DAD, HAVING A GOOD FAMILY."

Brady and Moynahan remained cordial privately and publicly, refusing to say anything bad about each other to the press. Moynahan raised their child, John, in New York City, while Brady lived in Boston and Florida and saw his son as often as he could during the football season. They spent their summers together. Even after he married Bündchen and they had two children of their own, John's presence was welcomed into their tight-knit and warm, if untraditional, family atmosphere.

SUCCESS CAN COME AT ANY AGE

By 2019, when he was 42, the age at which most professional football players have retired from the physical, grueling grind of the sport, it looked like Tom Brady may have peaked. At least the New England Patriots, his professional home for two decades, seemed to think so. In 2020, Brady and team executives negotiated a contract extension. Brady wanted a long-term, multi-year deal that would see him through to the end of his career, somewhere around age 45. The Patriots weren't willing to give one of the most expensive contracts in sports history to a player who could very well have passed his prime. It was true that his numbers had fallen off in 2019. While his stats

"THERE'S A LOT OF PEOPLE WHO DON'T LIKE TOM BRADY, AND I AM OKAY WITH THAT."

"I'M NOT GOING TO GIVE AWAY MY POWER. YOU CAN CALL ME AN [EXPLETIVE] AND I'M GOING TO SMILE AT YOU PROBABLY."

were still strong at 4,057 passing yards and an 88 quarterback rating, they weren't his best.

Brady believed he still had many highly productive, elite seasons left in him, so he resolved to walk away from the New England Patriots. He signed with the Tampa Bay Buccaneers instead. And he proved doubters, particularly those in the front office at the Patriots, incorrect. At age 43, his stats improved in Florida, with 4,633 passing yards, 40 touchdowns, and a 102.2 quarterback rating. At the conclusion of the 2020–21 season, his first with the Bucs, Brady would go on to prove himself right and his doubters wrong.

LIFE LESSONS FROM A LEGEND

- THERE IS A WIN IN EVERY DEFEAT IF YOU LOOK FOR IT.
- APPRECIATE GROWTH AMIDST SETBACKS AND LOSSES.
- LET YOUR STRUGGLES INSPIRE HARD WORK AND PASSION.
- STEER CLEAR OF DRAMA.
- IT'S NEVER TOO LATE TO ACHIEVE YOUR DREAMS.

DISCIPLINE MATTERS

Tom Brady is driven by a deep-seated desire to succeed at the highest level possible and to win. In order to achieve all that he knows he's capable of accomplishing, and at an elite level that pushes his body to its maximum potential, Brady has to prepare by committing to a strict daily regimen.

Brady is nothing if not detail oriented when it comes to work and preparation for games. He maximizes his strengths, works on his weaknesses, and directs his limited time and energy with a personal daily playbook.

CREATE AND ADHERE TO A WINNING ROUTINE

Preparing for success involves rigorous organization. To maintain his physical, mental, and emotional health, and establish a work-life balance, all of which are necessary for performing at peak condition, he follows a strict routine that affects almost every element of his life.

"THE MORE GOOD BEHAVIORS YOU HAVE, THE BETTER THINGS TURN OUT."

At 5:30 a.m. on an average day during the NFL offseason, without any need for an alarm, Brady has conditioned himself to wake up and follow his meticulous schedule. After about two hours of vigorous cardiovascular exercise and weight training, he's back at home by 8 a.m. to enjoy breakfast and some unstructured time with his kids if they're with him. They might wander down to the beach near his home in Miami (he also has a place in Tampa near the Tampa Bay Buccaneers headquarters). At 11 a.m., Brady takes an hourlong nap, follows it up with an hour for lunch, and then spends the afternoon exercising again, whether that

STAT ⚡ Tom Brady is the NFL's all-time leader in completed passes, passing yards, and passing touchdowns.

"I THINK I'VE ALWAYS TRIED TO BE VERY PROFESSIONAL TO HOW I APPROACH THE GAME, MY PREPARATION. EVERY GAME IS IMPORTANT."

"SEE, THERE ARE
A LOT OF GUYS
WHO ARE ALL TALK.
THEY SAY THEY WANT
TO WORK HARDER
AND BE THE BEST,
BUT THEY NEVER
PAY THE PRICE."

"I ALWAYS TRY TO DO AS MUCH AS I CAN DO. I'M NEVER A PERSON THAT DOES NOT ENOUGH."

means surfing or working out at the gym. At 6 p.m., he has dinner and spends some time reviewing game film and developing game strategy either on his own or with one of his coaches. By 8:30 p.m., Brady is asleep.

EAT TO FUEL YOUR LIFE

Brady depends on his body to work as reliably and efficiently as possible, so he is extremely selective in what he consumes. Through his former teammate, linebacker Willie McGinest, Brady met Alex Guerrero, a personal trainer and expert in natural medicine and nutrition. Together, they developed a personalized eating plan for Brady called the TB12 diet.

Thanks to Gisele's influence, he'd already been adhering to a mostly plant-based, animal products-free diet since 2015. The TB12 diet is a similarly vegetarian-oriented plan heavy on nutrient-rich, organic, and locally sourced foods. The TB12 diet consists of 80 percent alkaline and 20 percent acidic foods, meaning it's heavy on leafy green vegetables and protein shakes made from plant-based

"I DON'T EVEN ENJOY EATING THINGS THAT PROBABLY AREN'T GOING TO GIVE MY BODY WHAT IT NEEDS."

sources. He doesn't eat a lot of wheat or grains, and eschews any fruits that aren't berries, because berries are lower in sugar than most fruits and are full of healing antioxidants. He gets a lot of his protein from nuts and avocados. During the winter, or the NFL season, when his body requires more protein, iron, and nutrients, he does eat animal products like fish and beef.

Brady believes that his diet limits inflammation and promotes internal chemical reactions that help his body stay fit for high-level performance in the NFL. He commits himself to this daily regimen because he believes it allows for greater muscle pliability and flexibility, and faster recovery after workouts, games, and collisions. According to Brady, it also affords him extra energy. Shortly after adopting the diet in his late thirties, Brady found that he was actually able to run faster than he had in previous years, and speed has been an area he's been trying to improve upon since high school.

STAT ⚡ With Tom Brady at starting quarterback, neither the New England Patriots nor the Tampa Bay Buccaneers have ever had a season where they lost more games than they won.

"WINNERS FOCUS
ON WINNING.
LOSERS FOCUS
ON WINNERS."

MIND GAMES

In addition to staying hydrated and getting plenty of sleep each night to keep his brain fully functioning, Brady plays brain-stimulating video games on his laptop and tablet computer. They encourage quick thinking and object identification, skills he hones for on-field work, like spotting open receivers or avoiding approaching linebackers. Brady personally met with the makers of BrainHQ, a system used to help people who suffered from traumatic brain injuries recover from memory loss and cognitive damage.

He says that he plays more than two dozen brain games every day, and that they help him develop and maintain memory, processing, and focus. They also help him relax after a game.

The TB12 diet requires more than a few sacrifices: Brady isn't allowed to eat tomatoes, processed foods, most oils, coffee, MSG, soy, corn, dairy, or gluten. But he considers it a small price to pay on the way to his goals.

"I DON'T WANT TO GIVE OFF THE IMPRESSION THAT I'M SOME PSYCHOPATH ABOUT A DIET. I JUST MAKE GOOD CHOICES MOST OF THE TIME."

"I WASN'T BORN A PRODIGY, LIKE A 3-YEAR-OLD THE WORLD BESTOWED GREATNESS ON."

TRAIN YOUR BRAIN

Making yourself into a champion, a person capable of legendary status, is an all-encompassing endeavor. Tom Brady knows that mental training is as crucial to success as physical training. For quarterbacks in particular, football requires lightning-quick decision-making skills made in the heat of the moment and sometimes in the clutch final seconds of a game. For championship athletes, the rollercoaster of highs and lows requires unfailing confidence. Mental training means, in part, nurturing that confidence and adapting your thinking to pave the way for future success.

Mental toughness, the ability to maintain a positive outlook no matter what challenge you face, is a core component of Brady's formula for success. It's essential for him to rebound from difficult situations and avoid dwelling on past mistakes. As Brady defines it, "Mental toughness is centered on doing the best you can in the present while believing you can do even better in the future." He doesn't believe in playing the victim or making excuses for his mistakes. That brand of negativity hasn't proven as useful to him or as empowering as positivity.

PUSH YOURSELF

The physical workout that Tom Brady sticks to is expertly designed

"OUTSIDE OF PLAYING FOOTBALL, THE ONE THING I LOVE TO DO IS TO PREPARE FOR IT."

by his team of trainers for maximum performance and to keep his body working at full efficiency and minimize wear and tear. The individual exercises are tailor-made to ensure that he can play football at a high level into his forties without sustaining injuries.

During the football season, Brady's physical fitness begins as soon as he wakes up. First, he drinks 20 ounces of water infused with nutrients and electrolytes. Water is vitally important to Brady's health. (He drinks as many as 25 glasses a day.) Before he begins his gym workout, he puts in a pre-workout pliability session, priming the muscles that allow him to move and throw with precision and grace on the field. After a two-hour workout, consisting of nine strength, conditioning, and speed-boosting

"MY BODY STILL FEELS LIKE I'M IN MY 20S."

"THERE ARE
NO SHORTCUTS
TO SUCCESS
ON THE FIELD
OR IN LIFE."

"I REALLY DO JUST WANT TO WIN, AND THAT HAS AND WILL CONTINUE TO BE THE REASON THAT MOTIVATES ME."

exercises, many of which involve the use of strong resistance bands and emphasize strengthening his core and throwing arm, he'll put in another pliability session. From there, he'll head to team practice, where he'll perform more muscle conditioning exercises.

TAKE A WHOLE-BODY APPROACH

Brady takes a holistic approach to health and rounds out his regimen with soothing and healing practices like yoga, meditation, and massage. Grounding himself in this way helps him feel more prepared and calm heading into stressful games or situations.

What's most insightful about the daily work that Brady puts into his mind and body is that he doesn't consider it work. He found what he loves to do, and he intends to do it for as long as possible. Early in his career, Brady floated the

---

STAT ⚡ Tom Brady is the oldest NFL Most Valuable Player ever at age 40, the oldest Super Bowl MVP at 43, and the oldest quarterback selected to the Pro Bowl at age 44.

---

idea of playing until he was 40, and he set about making sure he would do that. But when 40 approached, he publicly proposed playing until 50, and he just might get there thanks to his dedicated, all-in approach to fitness, wellness, and life in general.

LIFE LESSONS FROM A LEGEND

- DEVELOP A DAILY, GOAL-ORIENTED ROUTINE.
- MAKE TIME FOR EVERYTHING THAT MATTERS.
- TREAT YOURSELF AND YOUR BODY RIGHT.
- PRIORITIZE YOUR MENTAL HEALTH AND OVERALL WELLNESS.
- MAKE A PLAN FOR SUCCESS.
- WITH ENOUGH DISCIPLINE AND DETERMINATION, YOU CAN MEET YOUR GOALS.

"WHEN I PLAY FOOTBALL, I APPRECIATE IT. I AM NOWHERE ELSE, I AM IN THE PRESENT."

PLAY BY YOUR OWN RULES

The dream of becoming the best pro football player has been the driving force of Tom Brady's life. He achieved that goal and then some, elevating himself through hard work over many decades into a true legend. But once a person reaches their goals and fulfills their dreams, what comes next? If they're like Brady, they reflect and expand their vision to go beyond that singular ambition and share their success with others. Brady, after winning all those Super Bowls and making millions of dollars, resolved to give back to those who helped make him who he became—particularly his family, his spouse, his children, and his community.

HELP THOSE WITH LESS

Expanding on the name and goals of his long-term health and nutrition business, Brady created the TB12 Foundation in 2015. A charitable organization, it aims to help athletes who are disadvantaged in some way (economically or physically) secure athletic performance training and intensive post-injury care and conditioning. Brady's foundation operates two free medical facilities, one in suburban Boston (near where he played with the Patriots) and one in Tampa (near his home playing with the Buccaneers). The TB12 Foundation seeks to help injured athletes of all ages and focuses some of its efforts on active-duty military members, retired military veterans, and first responders, including paramedics and firefighters.

Brady spends a lot of time working with and promoting charities and nonprofit groups that share his values. One of them is KABOOM!, an organization that builds playgrounds for kids in underserved or economically disadvantaged urban areas. A nonprofit organization close to Brady's heart is Best Buddies International, a group that strives to encourage a better understanding of people with developmental and intellectual challenges through one-to-one

friendships and social outreach programs. Brady's work with Best Buddies has led to $45 million in fundraising over 20 years. He's also an active fundraiser for the Boys and Girls Clubs of America, a network of afterschool community centers for kids and teens.

HONOR YOUR ROOTS

Time and time again, Tom Brady has shown his appreciation for his family and the institution that first believed in him. In 2012, Brady returned to Junipero Serra High School in San Mateo, California, to be the keynote speaker at the institution's Fund a Dream Scholarship Benefit. Brady personally donated $100,000 in scholarship funds as well as two signed game jerseys, which earned another $40,000 for the school at auction. After a subsequent donation, the school renamed its sports facility after Brady, its most famous and notable graduate. Brady, surprisingly, didn't approve and instead requested that the stadium name include his talented sports-achieving siblings. Later that year, the Brady Family Stadium was officially christened.

STRIVE FOR BALANCE

Tom Brady has two priorities in his life: his children and football. With his ex-wife Gisele Bündchen, he is raising their kids, Benjamin (born in 2009) and Vivian (born in 2012), and often bring Jack, Brady's son from his previous relationship with actress Bridget Moynahan, into the fold. In 2010, before his daughter was even born, his values were clear:

> *"I love coming to work every day. But also, being at home, and giving those boys my attention, and my affection, and my discipline, and being a good parent is so important, because I grew up with two of the best parents a son could ever ask for."*

Like many other adults with a family and a demanding, time-consuming job, Brady struggled to balance the demands of home life and work life. He knew that his job had the tendency to be all-consuming: "I think I make a lot of—I wouldn't call them sacrifices, but just concessions for my job."

Brady was at times so committed to football that he had to reassess his personal life. In the 2010s, then-wife Bündchen wrote Brady a letter, telling him that he had been neglecting his duties as a family man:

> *"She felt like I would play football all season, and she would take care of the house. And then, all of a sudden, a season would end, and I'd be like 'Great, let me get into all my other business activities. Let me get into my football training.' And she's sitting there going, 'Well, when are you going to do things for the house? When are you going to take kids to school and do that?' That was a big part of our marriage that I had to check myself."*

"THE POINT OF A RELATIONSHIP, IT HAS TO WORK FOR BOTH. YOU BETTER WORK ON BOTH BECAUSE IF YOU DON'T, ULTIMATELY, IT'S NOT SUSTAINABLE."

He worked on finding a new approach to balancing the competing demands of family and career. In response to his wife's concerns that he wasn't spending enough time or effort on his personal life, he scaled back his offseason football training regimen and agreed to enter into marriage counseling with Bündchen.

DO YOU, AND FOR AS LONG AS POSSIBLE

As early as 2018, Bündchen had been trying to get her husband to retire from football. Immediately after the Super Bowl in 2021, which the then-43-year-old Brady won for a record seventh time, she asked him on the field, while their

LETTERS TO LIVE BY

Brady's family motto is CCC, which stands for "clear, current communication." It means you should express your feelings in the present moment to address problems or concerns.

"I LOVE WHAT I DO, AND I WANT TO DO IT FOR A LONG TIME."

MONEY MAKERS

Tom Brady has earned more than $300 million in NFL salary alone. His standing $375 million deal with Fox Sports to become a lead NFL analyst is the most lucrative deal in sports broadcasting history.

children hugged him and celebrated, "What more do you have to prove?" Brady knew she wanted him to spend more time with his family, but he opted to play another year for the Tampa Bay Buccaneers.

After winning 13 games in that regular season, the Bucs lost in the divisional playoffs to the Los Angeles Rams, 30-27. Brady retired, officially ending his monumental 22-year NFL career:

> *"I made the decision in the moment, and I felt it was the right thing for the team to let the Bucs know. You need time to plan. And then through conversations with Bruce [Arians, the team's former coach], Jason [Licht, general manager] and my wife, I felt like I could still play and compete."*

Just 40 days later, he unretired and committed to playing at least one more year of professional football.

This move would put added strain on his relationship with his wife. In October of 2022, their marriage ended in divorce. Football clearly had a firm hold on Brady. As he explained in an interview with WEEI in 2019, he struggled with the notion of letting it go:

> *"I don't know, it's just some people are maybe great guitarists, there's great chefs, there's great lawyers, there's great artists, actors, you name it. I think if you really love it, why should you stop? You just love it. I don't know how to explain it other than I love doing it and that is enough for me."*

"I JUST HAVE A
COMPETITIVE FIRE
THAT GOT THE
BEST OF ME."

While he did officially retire on February 1st, 2023 at age 44, Brady was not about to leave the sport entirely. He was eager to try out his new role as an NFL commentator.

Brady can't put out the fire that fuels him. He steps into every arena ready to humbly and wholeheartedly accept the challenges ahead. This next era of his career will be no different. He has proven his status as a football legend and a worthy mentor again and again, but when you're as driven as Tom Brady, the job is never done.

LIFE LESSONS FROM A LEGEND

- IF YOU'VE BEEN SUCCESSFUL AND LUCKY IN YOUR ACHIEVEMENTS, PAY IT FORWARD.
- BE THERE FOR YOUR KIDS AND YOUR COMMUNITY.
- LIVE UP TO YOUR OWN STANDARDS.
- IF YOU FIND SOMETHING YOU LOVE TO DO, DON'T GIVE IT UP WITHOUT A FIGHT.

I STILL HAVE MORE TO PROVE

"I just wanted to say to all of our fans, THANK YOU!

After a few days of reflection, I am so grateful and humbled by the unconditional support you have shown me the past two decades. Running out of that tunnel every week is a feeling that is hard to explain. I wish every season ended in a win, but that's not the nature of sports (or life). Nobody plays to lose. But the reward for working hard is just that, the work!! I have been blessed to find a career I love, teammates who go to battle with me, an organization that believes in me, and fans who have been behind us every step of the way.

Every one of us that works at Gillette Stadium strived to do their best, spent themselves at a worthy cause, and prepared to fail while daring greatly (h/t Teddy Roosevelt). And for that, we've been rewarded with something that the scoreboard won't show—the satisfaction of knowing we gave everything to each other in pursuit of a common goal.

That is what TEAM is all about.

In both life and football, failure is inevitable. You don't always win. You can, however, learn from that failure, pick yourself up with great enthusiasm, and place yourself in the arena again.
And that's right where you will find me. Because I know I still have more to prove."

—Tom Brady, Instagram post, January 8, 2020

RESOURCES

MAGAZINES/WEBSITES/ NEWSPAPERS

"5 Career Lessons to Learn from Tom Brady"
Inc., January 31, 2019

"21 things you might not have known about Tom Brady"
Insider.com, February 1, 2022

"After Stellar NFL Career, Tom Brady Leaves Behind Leadership Examples And Lessons"
Forbes, February 1, 2022

"Buccaneers restructure QB Tom Brady's contract to create $9M in cap space"
NFL.com, April 22, 2022

"By the numbers: Most insane Tom Brady stats and facts"
The Wolverine, February 4, 2022

"Day in the Life: Tom Brady"
Owaves.com, February 4, 2022

"Deflategate timeline: After 544 days, Tom Brady gives in"
ESPN.com, September 3, 2015

"Depth Chart"
Patriots.com, August 22, 2000

"Draft Review: Tom Brady—the GOAT? Not back in 2000"
Sports Illustrated, June 21, 2021

"Gisele Bündchen comforts children after Patriots' Super Bowl loss, congratulates Eagles"
USA Today, February 5, 2018

"Gisele Rides Again"
Elle, Sept. 13, 2022

"How does Tom Brady keep winning Super Bowls? It might have more to do with his brain than you think"
CNBC, February 4, 2019

"Is this the end for Tom Brady? Relive the legend's high school career"
USA Today, January 30, 2022

"Jerry Rice, Tom Brady, and Lawrence Taylor top our list of the 100 greatest NFL players of all time"
USA Today, October 1, 2019

"Living Like Tom: One *Sports Illustrated* Writer Takes On the TB12 Method"
Sports Illustrated, July 26, 2017

"Look Back at Tom Brady and Bridget Moynahan's Rocky Relationship"
Us Weekly, March 14, 2022

"More of Brady's chat with Tirico"
ESPN.com, December 9, 2012

"Motivational Tom Brady Quotes About Football and Life"
On3.com, April 19, 2022

"Motivational Tom Brady Quotes to Help You Unleash Your Inner Legend"
TheSTRIVE.co, May 23, 2022

"NFL: Records from 2016 don't show Tom Brady had or complained of concussions"
ESPN.com, May 17, 2017

"Oldest NFL players in history: Where does Tom Brady rank on all-time list?"
Sportingnews.com, October 3, 2021

"Patrick Mahomes was among the first players to congratulate Tom Brady on Super Bowl win"
USA Today, February 7, 2021

"Patriots president: There 'wasn't one person who said' to hire Bill Belichick in 2000"
CBS Sports, February 21, 2017

"Perry: The 10 lessons learned on the Tom Brady beat"
NBC Sports, September 30, 2021

"Remembering Deflategate: What really happened? Did Tom Brady cheat with New England Patriots?"
USA Today, January 29, 2022

"Serra to name football stadium after Brady"
Mercury News, February 24, 2012

"Struggling with work-life balance? NFL superstar Tom Brady reportedly feels your pain"
Deseret News, August 12, 2022

"Surpassing Michael Jordan as ultimate GOAT is Tom Brady's last challenge"
ESPN.com, May 15, 2017

"Tom Brady"
IMDb.com, July 12, 2022

"Tom Brady"
Pro-Football-Reference.com
July 10, 2022

"Tom Brady and Gisele Bündchen's Marriage Troubles 'Have Been Going on Forever': Source"
People, October 7, 2022

"Tom Brady announces his retirement from the NFL after 22 seasons"
Sky Sports, February 7, 2022

"Tom Brady Calls Working Hard a 'Very Sustainable Trait'"
People, November 15, 2021

"Tom Brady Diet Plan: How Can You Win 7 Super Bowl?"
YebScore.com, July 4, 2021

"Tom Brady fell asleep before his first Super Bowl and woke up with minutes to spare before the team took the field"
Insider.com, January 11, 2019

"Tom Brady Gets Weepy, Cocky, And Downright Dark In Final Episode Of 'Man In The Arena' Docuseries"
CBS News Boston, April 26, 2022

"Tom Brady, Gisele Bündchen hire divorce lawyers amid marital woes: sources"
New York Post, October 6, 2022

"Tom Brady: 'Gisele Urged Me to Retire After SB'"
TMZ, March 3, 2021

"Tom Brady Just Received the Ultimate Compliment From His Head Coach After Leading the Buccaneers to the Super Bowl"
Sportscasting.com, January 25, 2021

"Tom Brady Life Lessons: Change Your Life In 2021 For Good"
YebScore.com, July 17, 2021

"Tom Brady 'Nearly Pulled Off the Greatest Comeback of His Career'"
Fox Sports, January 24, 2022

"Tom Brady officially announces retirement from NFL after 22 seasons"
NFL.com, February 1, 2022

"Tom Brady on eventual retirement: 'I've realized I don't have five years left'"
NFL.com, July 14, 2022

"Tom Brady on OMF discusses N'Keal Harry, what keeps him wanting to play until 45"
WEEI, November 13, 2019

"Tom Brady Opens Up About DeflateGate: 'I Don't Need To Defend Myself'"
CBS News Boston, December 31, 2021

"Tom Brady taking leave of absence from Tampa Bay Buccaneers to 'deal with personal things'"
CNN, August 12, 2022

"Tom Brady's Acceptance Speech After Winning Sportsperson of the Year"
Sports Illustrated, December 7, 2021

"Tom Brady's Former Teammate Wanted to Hate Him When He Joined the Patriots: 'He's Feeding Me Some BS'"
Sportscasting.com, August 19, 2021

"Tom Brady's Game Plan: The Legend on Why He Won't Set a Retirement Date, Making Movies and His $375 Million Fox Sports Deal"
Variety, July 14, 2022

"Tom Brady's Intense Routine That Keeps Him Fit"
HealthDigest.com, October 18, 2021

"Tom Brady's Legendary Leadership Boils Down to 3 Simple Words and a Humble Handshake"
Sportscasting.com, February 20, 2021

"Tom Brady's most dangerous game"
ESPN, October 31, 2017

"Tom Brady's Patriots contracts through the years"
NBC Sports, July 15, 2022

"Tom Brady says being called the 'GOAT' makes him cringe"
New York Post, February 5, 2019

"Tom Brady to join Fox Sports as network's lead NFL analyst after his playing days end"
Boston Globe, May 10, 2022

"The (Un-Retired) Quarterback and the Supermodel! Find Out All About Tom Brady's Marriage to Gisele"
Parade, March 13, 2022

"The Wake Up Call That Sent Gisele Bündchen And Tom Brady To Counselling"
Women's Health, August 27, 2020

"Why Tom Brady left the Patriots"
SBNation.com, February 6, 2021

BOOKS

12 Lessons in Business Leadership: Insights From the Championship Career of Tom Brady, by Kevin Daum

Brady vs Manning: The Untold Story of the Rivalry That Transformed the NFL, by Gary Myers

The Game of Eating Smart, "Nourishing Recipes for Peak Performance Inspired by MLB Superstars" by Julie Loria

The TB 12 Method: How to Achieve a Lifetime of Sustained Peak Performance, by Tom Brady

Tom Brady: Football Superstar, by Matt Scheff

Tom Brady: The Game Is Your Life, by L. Davidson

Tom Brady: The Inspirational Story of Football Superstar Tom Brady, by Bill Redban

Tom Brady: The Inspiring Story of One of Football's Greatest Quarterbacks, by Clayton Geoffreys

Who Is Tom Brady?, by James Buckley, Jr.

OTHER MEDIA

Man in the Arena: Tom Brady, ESPN Films, 2021–2022

"TO ANYONE WHO IS
STRUGGLING EARLY IN THE
MORNING OR LATE AT NIGHT
IN PURSUIT OF YOUR DREAM,
STRUGGLES THAT MANY WILL
NEVER SEE, AND TO ANY
LEADERS OUT THERE,
WHO BELIEVE IN SOMEONE
WHO DOES NOT YET
BELIEVE IN THEMSELVES,
KEEP GOING . . ."